I can do all things!

I0418155

I can do it!
I am kind.
I am helpful.
I am focused.

This notebook belongs to:

I am unstoppable.
I am thankful.
I am polite.
I am awesome!

Copyright © 2022 C. A. M Jackson
All rights reserved.
Made in Brooklyn.

ISBN: 979-8-9851561-1-9

I have so much value!

I am loved.

My voice matters.

I will control my happiness.

I am
powerful.

I learn from my mistakes.

I am
brave.

I am not afraid of a challenge.

My future is bright.

Today will be a great day.

I am
enough.

I am grateful for what I have.

I am
a leader.

I am good at a lot of things.

I am a
good
person.

I choose to focus on what I can control.

I am kind
to others.

I am special in my own way.

There is
no one
like me.

I will make a difference in the world around me.

I believe
in myself.

I stand up for what I believe in.

_____

_____

_____

_____

_____

_____

_____

_____

_____

_____

_____

_____

_____

_____

_____

_____

I am a
honest
person.

I am confident in myself.

I am
smart.

I am open to new experiences.

My
opinions
matter.

I am in charge of my happiness.

Each day is a fresh start.

I am proud of the things I have accomplished.

I deserve
to be
happy.

I will work hard to achieve my goals.

I accept
my
differences.

I will treat others the way I want to be treated.

_____

_____

_____

_____

_____

_____

_____

_____

_____

_____

_____

_____

_____

_____

_____

_____

_____

_____

I am a
good
listener.

Each day I work on being a better version of myself.

**I am
stronger
than I think.**

My thoughts and feelings are important.

Today will be a great day.

I love myself just the way I am.

I am wonderfully made.

I am not afraid to try new things.

**I am loved
just the
way I am.**

I can always try again
if I need to.

Mistakes help me grow.

My character matters.

I will speak
up for
myself.

I am learning new things about myself each day.

www.ingramcontent.com/pod-product-compliance
Lightning Source LLC
Chambersburg PA
CBHW070438130626

46553CB00006B/2238